Dark Things Still

Dark Things Still

Poems by

Philip Andrew Lisi

Cover design by Shay Culligan
Cover image *The Tree of Crows* by Caspar David Friedrich

ISBN: 979-8-90146-801-2
Library of Congress Control Number: 2026933204

Kelsay Books
502 South 1040 East, A-119
American Fork, Utah 84003
Kelsaybooks.com

For my father,
who read me my first poem
and taught me that, with love,
broken things can be redeemed

Acknowledgments

Thank you to the editors of the following publications in which many of the poems in this collection first appeared, sometimes in earlier versions:

Broad River Review: "Order of Operations"
Carolina Muse: "Pond Season"
Change Seven Magazine: "Broken Things," "Marigold in Your Absence"
Flora Fiction Literary Magazine: "Diner Love," "Measured in Hours," "No Place for Freya"
Friday Flash Fiction: "Old Friends"
Green Ink Poetry: "Magpies and Mortsafes"
HOOT: "Western Lanes"
Kelp Journal: "Fireflies"
Last Leaves Magazine: "A Winter Birthday"
MockingHeart Review: "Bullfrog"
October Hill Magazine: "Chrysanthemums After the Fall," "Marginalia"
Poetry Super Highway: "Human Nature," "Something New"
Scarlet Dragonfly Journal: "House on the Hill"
ScribesMICRO: "Lunar Light"
Sixfold: "Indelible at Dawn," "Upturned"
Sky Island Journal: "Electric Blue" (originally "Lisa"), "First Aid"
Sparks of Calliope: "Elegy," "Keepsakes" (originally "The Keeping"), "Dark Things Still" (originally "Not Killing a Spider")
Synkroniciti Magazine: "First Kiss"

The Orchards Poetry Journal: "Invasive Species," "Waiting in Winter"
Third Wednesday Magazine: "October in Adams County"
Wild Roof Journal: "Convergence"

Thank you to my fellow Arcadian poeteers—Amanda Conover, Justine Defever, Carol Smith, and Dameien Sykes-Bidwell—and to my mentors, Genevieve Betts and Michelle Reale. You are blessings to me, all.

Contents

Someone I loved once gave me
A box full of darkness.
It took me years to understand
that this, too, was a gift.

—Mary Oliver, "The Uses of Sorrow"

Midnight Menagerie

The Dutch rabbit
sits on the dresser,
head tilted down,
admiring the fur feathering
at the tips of her creme-colored toes
before her gaze falls upon

the gray fox,
wiry and wild-eyed,
proud of his voluminous tail
and maybe just a little bit wicked
as he looks across the room
to the desk where

the wombat lounges,
lazy and stout,
eyes closed,
claws resting across a broad belly,
satisfied without a care in the world,
yet his nose twitches,
sensing the proximity of

the ringtail,
whiskers like stiff corn silk
appearing just over the edge of the desk,
quivering in anticipation of mischief-making,
conscious that she is being surveilled
from the top of the corner bookcase by

the cat,
black as pitch,
standing sentinel,
watching with eyes of blue-green phosphor,
waiting for you to come home.

Electric Blue

You know those popsicles, advertised in the window
as *Twin Pops!* at the PennSupreme
on the corner of Fountain and Martha?
Blue raspberry—*electric blue,* you called it,
as your eyes lit up in blue flame to match.

There was a freezer full of them in your pool house,
always stocked with ice cream sandwiches
and Dixie Cups with the little wooden spoons attached
like miniature canoe paddles.

Any of these frozen confections would have
satisfied my six-year-old sweet tooth,
but when you pulled out the box of twin pops
and said—*These are my favorite!*
any deliberation on my part was short-lived.
At that moment, your favorite was my favorite.

Just about every Sunday afternoon that summer,
we drove across Wright's Ferry Bridge to swim.
You would hold me in the water, the support of your hands
barely perceptible as I practiced floating on my back.
At sixteen, you were older cousin, tender mother, crush.

In between impromptu swimming lessons—treading water,
beginnings of a breaststroke, semblance of a sidestroke—
we shared the cold-tongued bite of raspberry,
dissolving in an instant as your hand
caught a drop of blue on my cheek.

A Winter Birthday

My mother's apron was always red on birthdays,
starched and tied in the back with precision,
a perfect pair of loops,
one ribbon mirroring the other,
like little scarlet whips,
perfect for this year's circus-themed party.

I knew they were not really for me.
They were for the neighbors and other adults worth impressing
with a dizzying array of birthday party decor—
streamers in rainbow colors, crisscrossing the dining room,
napkins with clown faces, with the same wide smiles
worn by those gathered around the table,
balloons of blue, green, and yellow arrayed along the walls
and some in the corners where the hot air from vents in the floor
cause them to sway like floating heads of party guests.

I want to run to the basement
where sound is cool and color muted—
but am stuck at a table full of harlequins,
the chairs are arranged too tightly around.
Behind my mother there is a window,
and the panes are covered in frost, like layers of icy spiderwebs.

It gives me something else to think about
instead of the too-blue icing of the elephant,
who balances on a bright yellow ball at the center of the cake.

She lights the candles now, and there is a hush in the room—
a moment of silence before the singing begins.
In the reflection behind her, the ribbons dance like fire,
turning the icy patterns on my window to tears.

First Kiss

You stand tiptoe in front of the mirror,
pucker your lips, and kiss the air
just like Wesley taught you in *The Princess Bride,*
though more duckbill than dashing and hardly a kiss
rated *the most passionate since the invention of the kiss.*
Not like that, you hear Francis advise
from the door to the bedroom you share.
In the mirror, cheeks flush with heat
knowing someone saw.

Little brother, let me show you how it's done, he says,
as he takes his old Ace Frehley t-shirt from the floor
and wipes the steam collecting on the mirror.
You don't have to show me. I've kissed plenty of girls before.
Oh, yeah? Like who?
Margaret Fasnacht, at lunch recess.
In first grade? That doesn't count. Here, like this—
You try your best to match him,
marking the curve of his Cupid's bow,
noting the space between his face and the mirror.

Margaret Fasnacht materializes, a vapor in the foggy glass.
Her eyes close. Steady now—
the condensation is warm as your lips
barely brush her cheek. *How was that?*

But Francis has gone to the kitchen for a sandwich,
and Margaret Fasnacht dissolves
into droplets still suspended in the air.
You taste Ivory soap on your tongue and remember
how she laughed the day you told her you *didn't know how,*
while the other boys hit home runs, scored goals,
and knew nothing of loss.

Measured in Hours

My grandfather's John Deere lawn tractor
was a 420 model with special modifications—
a steel platform bolted onto the front end,
wide enough for three five-gallon buckets of mulch,
and a suction hose that feeds into the grass catcher,
secured by two blaze-orange bungee cords
from Hostetter's Hardware.
It's still there in his shop across from the house.

When school let out for the summer,
all I wanted to do was mow with Papa.
I can picture him now—always smiling,
puffing on a cheap El Producto or Dutch Masters cigar
from Sloan's Pharmacy.
I never saw him on the tractor without one,
as though it were a key to start the engine—
gasoline and a cigar.

Mother would always worry—
It's too dangerous! Watch those blades!
My sister wouldn't go near it—but I was never afraid.
Papa was right there with me,
invincible together as we mowed our way
around oaks and sycamores.

The 420 had to be repaired this summer.
A new drive shaft, the mechanic said.
Wears out after so many thousands of hours of mowing.

A John Deere's life isn't measured in miles like a car—
it's measured in hours.
I never noticed until after he was gone,
but there's a gauge for it in the green of the dashboard,
marking time with Papa,
a meter of incalculable love.

Cruelty

At first, it was indistinguishable
from the sound of the mower in the distance,
a vibration in the windowpanes,
as the drone of the engine dissipated
around the corner of the old science wing—
a chant punctuated with a laughter
on the wrong side of glee—
Benjamin Blantz pissed his pants!

Benjamin stood just outside the circle of boys.
He watched the cicada's wings
skitter across the blacktop
as Billy Swearingen looked to the crowd,
hungry as any marauding locust,
telling the crowd what it felt like to
rip that stupid bug's wings off.

After school, the chant followed him home—
first worming its way along the sidewalk trampled
upon by the Barkley boys,
then filling the porch where the house key
might have meant relief.

Benjamin knew otherwise.

As he reached into his jacket pocket
and gently pulled out the pair of wings,
framed in greenish black,
delicately held in transparent foil,
he could still hear the chant in the schoolyard—

Benjamin Blantz pissed his pants!
but the sound was different now—
singular and deafening—
the growl of his father's Camaro
as he formed a hollow in his fist
around wings of glass.

Marginalia

You had the most beautiful handwriting,
elegant and precise in its execution.
But it was not what you said in words
that I remember so vividly.

Illuminating your correspondences were whimsical scenes,
populated with creatures that became your signature—
a black cat skulking atop familiar letterhead,
a downy opossum, a row of pin-toothed passengers on her back,
a tawny field mouse, satisfied amidst hulls of cracked corn.

Just to the right of your name, a self-portrait,
no more than five or six exuberant squiggles of your pen,
your inky curls like tiny springs,
reminding me not to take myself too seriously.

The last time I saw you, you were writing something
on plain white stationery embossed with a rose.
You showed it to me and smiled—
but the tumor in your brain
had changed your familiar hand
into something unintelligible.

Still, I saw love in the margins,
and that is what I think of first on Thanksgiving,
the day you died—
your boundless light,
your curls radiant in their defiance
of the dark words metastasizing
outward from the center of the page.

No Place for Freya

> *Nature is in crisis because of us, but we do not seem to care . . . there is no room for Freya in Norwegian waters.*
>
> —Eurogroup for Animals

Freya was named for the Norse goddess of love and beauty. Ironic for a walrus weighing over a thousand pounds, wearing a gash in her left flipper, sporting a pink clam-shaped tattoo imprinted on her nose, and tusks so small as to be incidental. Her heavily whiskered countenance made her a charming plus-size pinniped from the Great White North, more Dolly Dimples than Marilyn Monroe.

She delighted onlookers with her antics, chasing ducks and clambering awkwardly onto pleasure boats, almost sinking them, basking in the summer sun of Oslo Fjord.

We watched, lustful behind sexy optics. We fed on social media and dined on selfies while you foraged for food in Frognerkilen because your regular invertebrate fare has been decimated as oil companies have darkened your normal feeding ground.

Just like us, then, to want to possess you, make it about us, driven by a voyeurism not limited to sideshows and roadside pleasure houses. Like a murmuration of maritime paparazzi, we did what we seem to do to just about everything—infringe, snap, capture, feed, displace, occupy.

Late one night in August, Freya was shot by four men who decided she was a burden to the local marina and posed a risk to children who might get too close. Freya died on her name's day—Frjádagr, Friday.

In a veterinary institute, Freya's body was dismembered, samples of her blood taken, the rest of her dissolved in a vat of lye.

Chrysanthemums After the Fall

After Vanessa Bell's *Chrysanthemums*

We are here with what is left—
Bell's bird—a goldfinch, perhaps—
wearing a coat of blue,
turned upward toward the lip of the vase that holds them—
three chrysanthemums,

But my eye is taken not by the flowers here,
variegated in pink and red and white.
It is what is to the right of the vase that intrigues me most,
frightens me, even, so that, for a moment,
I cannot seem to feel the page under my fingertips.

Its iridescence and pattern are apparent to me—
purple and black at the center,
double-outlined with oxblood
and muted gold, scaly with age,
something dead but venomous still.

It is serpentine, that swath of exquisite silk
that runs the length of the vase.
I think, whatever it was while alive,
it has taken something from the blooms.

What will they do now,
still petalled and upright?

Maybe the snake has only shed his skin
and will come back again
and again and again.

And what of the bird?
A tiny golden aegis
against all that swallowing?
Will it be enough?

Will it be enough?

Diner Love

The top of the Heinz ketchup bottle at the Neptune Diner looked secure—I am sure it was on tight. But as I stare at the tomatoey Rorschach splotch adorning the front of your date-night dress, I guess I must have misjudged the synchronicity between white metal top with its spiral grooves and the striated glass of the neck. There must have been misalignment somewhere to allow for such chromatic chaos on periwinkle poplin. *I am so sorry. Send me the dry-cleaning bill. How else can I make it up to you?* Then, from behind the counter, two rice puddings in glass towers made for sundaes, whipped cream like fluffy white spires on *La Sagrada Familia,* arrive with a wink and a *on the house.* And you? *I love rice pudding,* you say, as you paint the red stain over your heart and into mine.

Dark Things Still

Yesterday, my colleague in the room next door
reported a sighting—
So disgusting! The ones that look like baby tarantulas.
Horrifying. I kill them on sight.

I am seated at my desk when you arrive,
feel you before I see you—
an uncanny sensation of weight
and dread in the air, then nothing—
but I know you are there,
and I cannot find my next breath.

Now I see you—
black mass of eight-legged menace,
and I consider my colleague's quick solution—
the crush and crunch of dominion,
and this appeals for a moment—
but two of your eight segmented limbs,
the pair framing what I take for your head,
positioned on either side of venomous black scythes,
reach gently, slowly, into the air,
as I hear my father's voice—
Spiders are friends.

My father never discarded things unnecessarily,
spiders or otherwise—
closet full of old tennis shoes fortified with duct tape,
baskets stacked with remnants
of worn-out red plaid pajamas for dusting,
a toolbox filled with shards of bar soap

others would have thrown away
without a thought as to their second life as
material for coating wood screws.

This is how he cultivated his peace,
his place in the world,
and spiders were friends—
even the ones I imagined lurked
in the recesses of the cellar,
watching from little lairs of dust and shadow.

I have tried to see the world as my father did,
as he so wanted me to see it—
a place of good hearts and mercy
and potential for repair
and new uses and purposes and lives.

Yet, then, as now, I could not help but notice
the dark things in the corners of the cellar—
ancient, otherworldly things,
alien to waxed floors and artificial light—
or any light at all.

I am not my father,
and I see dark things still—
but, as you raise and lower your arms,
considering something in the air,
I find my breath again
in your return to the liminal
beyond desk and wall.

Something New

You never had a pet growing up—
not a hamster, not even a goldfish
won at the fly-by-night carnival operation
that breezes through town every August.
So, when you asked, *What about a kitten?*
and looked at me with a look that outdid
Clarice or Faline or any other doe-eyed creature
Disney could dream up, I acquiesced,
hoping something new and fluffy and alive
would bring you back from three months ago
when I found you on the floor in the bathroom
holding something wrapped in pink terry—
too small, too still, too precious,
and not to be.

October in Adams County

We pick apples together as we have always done.
I watch you working the orchard rows,
balancing two in one hand, then another two,
so tender in your consideration of each variety.

Pink Lady, Pixie Crunch, Thornberry—
names that tingle in the back of the tongue.
Somewhere in the mix of Jupiter and Scarlet Crush
is Grimes Golden, sweet-tasting mother of Delicious.

When Eve suggested to Adam that he pick one to share,
it might have been a Stoke Red, Honeycrisp, or Virginia Beauty.
Then again, it may have been too hot in the Eden sun
to be thinking about making love.

Maybe she would have waited for a chill in air,
for a Fireside or SnowSweet that ripens later in the season,
then watched for his first blush,
tantalizing in those days of innocence.

You unload the last of the harvest,
Frostbite and Prairie Spy,
your arms dropping the bins straight down,
no sign of the gentleness from the morning.

In the evening, we stand at the kitchen counter,
cutting up quarters for sauce,
and I remember how you used to dance,
a blossom floating in the autumn air.

Threshold

My wife is in the kitchen,
and from where I am sitting in the next room,
I can see her setting the table.
Funny. There must be sound as she places the forks and the knives,
but I can't hear anything.
She moves soundlessly, thinking hard about something, I suspect.
Why can't I hear her?

It looks like you have a scar on your forehead, Daddy.
A scar?
My son follows me into the bathroom
to watch me,
to see if I will see what he sees.

I return to my rocking chair
and stare at the floor.
My wife has stopped working in the kitchen.
She is sitting now with her back to me. Still.

Don't worry, Daddy. It'll be okay tomorrow.
Like you tell me—things are always better in the morning.
Why don't I look up and accept his love?

Does he see what I see
at the threshold of the door,
the faint mark of reddish brown on oak?

My wife is still sitting,
silent and still in the kitchen,
the scrub brush and bucket deep within the sink
so he cannot see.

Perfecting Imperfection

The routine starts on Sunday
with a tiny flake of skin, barely detectable,
separating itself from the sturdier flesh
just underneath the edge of the fingernail.
I am careful, so very careful—
thumb and forefinger opposite, sliding under and over.

Now, deep breath—
pull up slightly and then back toward the wrist
the first metacarpal a needle on a compass,
a goal for this evening's session.
A little bleeding is okay—but too much, too deep
will be harder to mask with a bandage.

On Monday, when people ask—
What happened to your fingers?
I deflect with a quip about tangling
with an especially insidious patch of thistle.

On Tuesday, the thumbs are back in the rotation,
just about healed now.
A ten-day cycle works perfectly,
a ten-day course of micro mutilation,
just enough to take the edge off,
in full view with every hand gesture in the classroom,
but easier to explain away than long sleeves in August.

Plus, it feels good to show the world
that I would rather be the one in charge
of my own destruction and renewal,
one sliver at a time.

I have made it to Friday, and like most every Friday,
I think—*This time, it will heal just right. This time.*
Every week, I wish I could come back *just right,*
as though, somehow, stripping away parts of myself,
little by little, layer by layer,
I will come back whole, perfected for you.

Exhaustion

On Sunday morning,
I stepped out of church to call you,
left a message, texted you,
asked if you were okay.

Last evening, I rushed home
from a board meeting to stay with the kids
because you were headed out for the night.
Will you text me to let me know where you'll be? I asked.

On Saturday night,
I called the bar we used to frequent together
to ask the fiery-haired barkeep,
who used to know me,
if you were there and, if so,
in his professional opinion,
whether or not you'd be walking home.

Twice this week,
you did text me to tell me
you were thinking about me
and even signed off with *I do love you,*
which you have done before,
as though committing the words to text
just one more time would reassure us both.

Then, two days of *omw* after work,
followed by 20 minutes that turned into 120
while I picked up the kids, took our son to piano,
picked up *your* shirts from the cleaners,
called *your* mother about plans for the weekend
and made spaghetti that hung listlessly from my fork
because anything else I could have prepared
required chopping and made me tired
just thinking about it.

This morning,
I step away from the church service once more,
forgetting now how many times
I have removed myself,
interrupted something, taken away,
skipped, relegated, compromised—
all in a hope that is killing us.

I do love you.
I hear your voice, my love—
but I am tired of doing the work of two
and finding new ways to explain your absence
in a house where peace comes in vapor dreams
over boiling water for pasta,
when I can just about imagine
how you used to be.

The Academy

It is Friday afternoon, and the books
on the shelf behind my desk stand sentinel—
the *Riverside Shakespeare,* a behemoth of tradition,
a pilfered volume from the *Oxford English Dictionary*
labeled L-M leans into a tattered reprint of Fitzgerald's *Gatsby,*
the eyes on the front cover leer at me
from a fading blue background.

All of these texts bow to those on the top shelf—
editions three through nine of the *MLA Handbook.*
They hand down their commandments and consequences—
beheading for forgetting a heading and header,
shackles for shirking the duty of italicizing titles of books,
banishment for using the first person in formal writing,
drawing and quartering for misplacing commas and periods
outside the quotation marks at the end of a sentence!

On Monday morning, when I encourage my students—
Think outside the box! Be creative! Be your best selves!
will I also admit my hypocrisy, tell them the truth,
that sometimes I see comfort in convention and adherence,
that sometimes I pray for a life with rules that are easily followed,
no thinking involved?

Human Nature

I watch the glasswing butterfly,
transparent foil in flight,
and feel a certain release—

until I hear the crunch of the abdomen
my son has separated with violent delight.

I shiver.

It is too cold for August.

House on the Hill

Bluestone and marble
for your bride and her children.
She leaves as it burns.

Bullfrog

It lies in wait at the edge of the pond, placid water on this cool morning. Surely, it is time for hibernating, burrowing deep into silty layers of leaves. A black-capped chickadee dances along the lip of flagstone framing the water and mottled remains of the summer's lily pads. With a *blink-gulp,* she is gone—and I am not sure what I just saw. A grotesque behemoth, all mouth and hundreds of tiny dagger-teeth, a serrated gardening trowel intent on killing. A lunge, a subtle *snap-thud,* like a rubber band against a thick rug, a gulp of velvet hat and downy vest. During the spring thaw, I unearth Leviathan's carcass from the muck. From the feeder, songbirds chirp a requiem, then a fanfare. For a moment, I share their triumph, then shudder and want to turn away from the decay coming to the surface as I stare into a fractured mirror and am devoured by a grin.

Fireflies

I

Summers ago,
you ran wild in the yard,
giddy as a sprite, chasing after fireflies,
gathering lightning in a jar.

Years older than you,
and not nearly as enthusiastic
about conscripting insects for mood lighting,
I watched from a distance
as you disappeared into the playhouse
where you used to invite me to tea parties.

There you were safe,
fortified by cedar shingles
and Perma-Stone walls.
I could see you through the window,
setting the table with Winne-the-Pooh cups and saucers
brought down from the attic,
placing at its center the result of your evening labors—
a lantern made of captive stars.

II

The yard is full of them tonight—
a thousand little sparks,
alive and gone in an instant—
then alive again, night shining
against the silhouette of the playhouse
before fading once more.

Tonight, I wish more than anything
I could do more than wipe the dust
from the jar you left on the little table
all those years ago.
I wish more than anything
I could capture enough light to bring you back,
to see you, once again,
in the luminescent breath of a firefly.

Forsaking All Others

Your hazeline eyes
swirl with forever
as I turn to see your face.
Your lips speak empyrean promises.
A white streak curls
through autumn hair
like a ribbon of Olympian flame.
Unheeding the eclipsing of the sun,
we press ourselves together
and turn to stone.

First Aid

I found it on Monday morning
after moving the bed away from the wall,
convinced that the watch I had given you
on your sixteenth birthday had fallen from
the Hitchcock nightstand and concealed itself
behind the maple headboard.

The watch wasn't there,
but I did find a blue steel box with *First Aid*
stenciled in red paint on the front.
Inside, a tattered copy of the *U.S. Army Survival Manual,*
dog-eared pages marking the basics
of shelter building and edible plants

Beneath the manual were rows and rows
of every imaginable size of Band-Aid—
the jumbo size, the tiny two-inch size
I used to place around your pinky finger
after removing a small thorn from the barberry bush
that divided Old Man Strunk's yard from ours,
and five inches of tight cotton mesh, guaranteed sterile.

What I already knew wasn't there anymore were six rolls of gauze.
Those you had used up, maybe gradually,
since you turned fourteen and started to close and lock your door
more often and not always at night.

Sometimes, you would be home early from school,
before I got home from work.
Maybe a quiet house helped you concentrate on the cut
and focus on the pain replacing pain.

I'd like to think you were just trying to find a way to start again,
that after that last cut, you would heal into a better you.
Instead, two days before graduation,
you inked your arms in two perfect lines
as red as the cross on the steel box in my hands.

Marigold in Your Absence

I may never understand how
you could be so fond of a chicken.
I find them unappealing—
beady little marble eyes,
residual reptilian features,
scaly legs and clawed feet.

But you loved Marigold,
your caramel-feathered Sussex hen,
talked to her every morning
the summer before you walked out,
thanking her for her humble offering
of one dusty-brown egg,
giving her a scoop of millet,
replenishing her water,
spreading fresh sawdust in her coop.

I remember watching you in the mornings,
happy in your routine and Marigold in hers—
patrolling the yard, scratching at a beetle,
pecking at your shoelaces,
making her strange purring
that sounded like gratitude.

You told me once how you loved
holding her, your fingers nesting
in her soft downy undercoat,
her hollow bones offering
a sense of weightlessness
and the potential for flight.

It is the first morning without you,
and Marigold does not come out for her millet.
No *purr-ruck-cluck-cluck* to greet me,
no scaly gams on display
on the wooden runway of her roost.
Instead, her right leg is held against her breast,
her claw curled like a fist.
If you were here, you would talk to her, hold her,
pressing feathers into something like love.

Plain Sight

Turning onto Snake Hill Road, the air is thick.
Weathered gray interminable in the morning mist,
three silos stand ahead of me, almost invisible.
A familiar windmill, solitary and still,
signals a sharp curve is approaching.
Three Amish girls emerge at the end of a lane,
appearing as grainy silhouettes against a dark corn field,
black bonnets and dresses, white aprons,
lunch pails hanging from their wrists.
I take the curve in a slow arch and wave.
I would like to think we exchange smiles.
I pass a one-room schoolhouse, the trio's likely destination.
The girls move in unison, free from ornament, resolute.
For a moment, they are held in the rearview mirror,
and I feel as though I could be among them.
A sharp descent to the river erases the tableau.
As I enter the covered bridge at Pinetown,
I no longer dream the other side.

Upturned

I really have no love for squirrels.
Well, maybe the rambunctious red ones,
those feisty fur balls with ear tufts
like the tips of little flames,
puckish, bold, and just a tad wicked,
the Nutkin Beatrix Potter knew,
chittering and dancing in the face of imminent peril.

But the gray squirrels in my neighborhood,
minds addled from nibbling at lead paint
peeling from rotting shutters,
are more menacing than their gingersnap brethren.

Destroyers of pumpkins in fall, wreaths in winter,
geraniums and begonias in spring and summer,
ravenous for ripping and uprooting.
Even in burying acorns for a later meal,
they leave the yard riddled with holes.

No—no love at all for these rodent wrecking crews.

I am surprised, then, when I see your soft white belly
upturned, tiny paws and bottlebrush tail
flat and still against the road,
and feel something other than hate.

Keepsakes

On the third floor,
the air is particled with old life—
when children drew
broad-whiskered cats
and wrote leaden cursive
on lines of yellow tablet paper
the color of yarrow.

Mother keeps these things
carefully pressed together
in files labeled with our names,
preserving what we might have been.

Sometimes, I imagine
they whisper together,
these parchments of the past,
like papery wasps
inside a dusty lamp shade—
Do you remember
when the children were young
and belonged to her?

In winter, she ascends the stairs
to visit us in our youth,
reminding herself of a time
when keeping and filing
labored to fill a space
that would always be hollow.

After she is gone,
I must enter there,
and I find it hard to breathe.
Bound to sort through
what is left of us,

I am held between lives
captured in time on fading pages
and want to burn them—
if only to martyr those memories
that once sustained
the outlines of love.

With a Whisper

Her hair is like wisps of milkweed floss
falling from dragonfly wings,
transparent filaments,
palliative against her pale blue pillow,
follicles left thirsty,
fruitless in their search
for chromatic life.

Curl and bounce have succumbed
to fraying and brittleness,
no fullness left to frame her face,
just a chalky shading
that a breath could wipe away.

Waiting in Winter

> *There are things you can't reach. But you can reach out to them . . . the wind. The bird flying away. The idea of God.*
>
> —Mary Oliver

I hear the great horned owl again tonight.
Perhaps it is returning to its nest with its kill
or announcing itself to a potential mate.
Ignoring the January chill and foregoing my coat,
I walk into the cold to look for it
among the boughs of our ancient oak,
a shadowy colossus standing sentinel
at the corner of the yard.

I use a red-filtered flashlight
to avoid startling the owl
and will myself to see more than I do,
every second mistaking squirrel nests
for this brown-feathered Tiger of the Air,
perfectly patterned for camouflage and stealth,
wishing for movement and seeing
only static branches in y-shapes.
Nothing—now that I am standing here.

I want to meet the elusive raptor,
silent and singular,
and glimpse the face of God—
but I do not see the owl
no matter how long I wait.
Then—a sound breaks the silence—
just the neighbor's rusty weathervane
shifting in the wind.

Order of Operations

First Tuesday of every month for six,
I drive you to the hospital.
You enjoy riding in my truck,
seeing everything, even as your legs,
skeletal parentheses in denim,
might not be strong enough
to make the step up into the cab
after this latest round of chemotherapy.

Outside your house, I wait on your porch.
Always prompt, you appear at the door,
corners of your mouth accented with dried saliva,
math textbook tucked tightly under your arm,
the laminate peeling back from the edges,
no pocketbook, no cardigan
draped over your arm.
I suspect you know its precise dimensions
and calculated its mass
in proportion to your featherweight frame.

Inside the treatment room,
Rosen's Discrete Mathematics Teacher's Edition
holds your attention.

Perhaps there is comfort in the familiarity—
brackets, square roots, variables,
old friends to polynomials, a fleeting balm,
one last attempt to solve,
the calculus of cancer.

Last night, on the eve of your final treatment,
I think about how I cried over the same tattered text,
endless algebraic equations, sitting at your kitchen table,
mind wandering, wishing your oatmeal cookies
would somehow make the numbers make sense.
Now, abstract calculations take your mind away
from the discrete pain of the needle
and the drip that kills as it sustains.

Old Friends

I visit Thelma in the skilled care unit at Willow Valley. I have brought her the homemade lasagna she loves so much. When she sees me, she smiles and intends to say, *Thank you,* I think—but instead says, *You came all this way to give me this? Well, that was dumb.* I sit beside her. She glances toward the window and muses, *I like to listen for the Amish horses and buggies passing by.* We wait together. In a while, we might play dominoes or gin. I will watch her oxygen levels and listen for the sound of hooves.

Pond Season

First, a good cleaning—
drain most of the water.
The siphon method with an old garden hose
will do as for our pond.
I have to see what is left—
so many fish disappear over winter,
taken, perhaps, by an intrepid night heron
or lost in some underground channel I will never see.

Next, knee-deep into the muck—
two inches of leaves, oak and maple,
silty remnants of fall.
Clumps of waterlogged locust leaves
like soggy mats made of firefly wings
and hemlock needles milled by a thousand pebbles
come up and out by the shovel full.

Then, rebuilding—
replace the rocks split apart by January's ice storms.
Careful not to dislodge the submersible pump,
replaced last spring, still in good shape.
I lie flat on my stomach,
legs extending away from the pond's perimeter,
counterweight to reaching down at awkward angles
to resurrect a shelf of blue slate, sandstone, and granite,
asymmetrical steps descending into the gray-green water.

Finally, some new lilies—
by mid-July, flotillas for the frogs
that come up from the creek down at Vic Dohner's,
little peepers, glossy and bright green,
not the grotesque monsters that hide among the rushes
a little farther off at Bushong's Pond. They are not welcome.
Water hyacinth—bulbs and flowers shaped
like Goetze's Caramel Creams, twin-twisted plastic ends.

My knees ache as I enter the screen porch,
pull off muddy boots, make my way to the shower.
I hear my son's voice from upstairs—
today is warm enough to open the windows
and bear the weight above the water.
Ophelia had her rosemary and herbs of grace.
If I see the yellow center of the Queen of Whites in June,
that will be my Easter Sunday.

Western Lanes

In the allies of the Western Lanes,
the dents in the wood are so numerous
the floors seem to ripple
under the cosmic lights
of Friday's Disco Bowling,
striated with ribbons of color
like an oily aurora borealis.
Tonight, I cannot decide which I envy more—
the old men who have been bowling together
since high school or the shoes behind the counter,
the ease of friendship,
the leathery timelessness
among the lights and thunder.

Lunar Light

I awake to banging
against the old wooden window.
Something is hitting hard
against the screen,
but when I get out of bed
to look outside
there is nothing
until I sense a great whirring.
At last, there! alighting
against the rusted mesh—
a celestial being in pale green
with colossal wings,
two mirrored segments like harps.
The stillness of this lime-green angel
offers a glimpse of the hereafter.
As she clings to the window between us,
her eyespots see me.
I sit with her,
and a long, pale-green tail
tells me fairies are real,
divine light finding me
only in the dark.

Elegy

Your paws have always reminded me
of a ballerina's pointe shoes,
beauty in seal-brown silk.

You look at me with disdain
(as any self-respecting cat would)
as I gently scoop you up to help you climb
the last few steps to my office—
oh, excuse me—*your* office.

You yowl in protest—
your voice still strong—
and I wonder how a sound
that resonates with such ferocity
can come from such a frail body,
diminished to next to nothing
in a period of weeks.

Tantrum over, pride restored,
you sit at my feet as I write,
cerulean eyes fixated on my lap—
which is also yours.

I pause and let you know I love you—
and I remember when you were a kitten
and used to wait for me at top of the stairs,
perched regally in the manner
of your ancient sister, the sphinx,
before bounding down to meet me at the door.

You seem content this evening,
sitting with me at my desk,
and I can feel the little rumble
from deep in your chest against my own—
a purring of tiny timpani,
a fanfare of feline affection—
too proud for *andante con dolore.*

You look up at me—
old eyes framed by long whiskers
the color of clotted cream.
Do you know?

I hold you now—
my arms wrapped around your body,
your dainty, dark-socked feet
indignant in a final *pas de chat.*
Beautiful girl—
I do not want to let you go.

Indelible at Dawn

In early morning, I see the skunk—
ball of black-and-white whimsy,
sniffing the ground, looking for grubs
with singular focus, unaware of my gaze.

She pauses her culling of beetle and root,
flashes her pink tongue, tasting dew in the air.
I step out into the backyard without a sound
and do not close the door.

She wobbles my way, grazing my right foot,
pauses, then turns her head toward the open door.
Does her keen nose detect coffee brewing in the kitchen?
Do I wish her away or welcome her inside?

Strange angel! I know you cannot stay for me—
but oh, how the day brightens as you
scuttle along the side of the house,
a white streak indelible at dawn.

Invasive Species

I drift, slow backstroke,
past cattails shedding
downy wisps into blue above.
To my right, a splash-dive,
and you emerge—
ember-eyed loon,
spear beak, a black thorn.
Just an arm's length away,
enormous this close,
threatening now.
Your discordant call,
startles me.

Am I too close to your nest?
Have I disturbed your quest
for lake trout?
Is it just to tell me
I do not belong here?

Forgive me—

this is the only place
I want to be.

Broken Things

Tiny opossum dragging your back legs
across the road toward my porch,
I see you in the evening sun, an already strange sight.
I think there might be nothing
more desperate or devastating than to see you like this,
trying so hard to cross from one side of nothing to the other.

I use the first thing I can find to place you in—
a large black tub, tough like a tire
and useful for many things—
harvesting fruit or hauling firewood.

Some call you ugly, rat, rodent, pest—
but you are beautiful,
fur glittering in the twilight,
triangle face striped with white tears.
Your mouth opens for a moment in a quiet hiss.
Black marble eyes and curled pink tail,
body in semicircle,
a crescent moon cradled in shadow.

I offer you water,
find a cricket, and hope you will eat it.
I place a call and am told
the wildlife rehabilitator
will come in the morning
to rescue you and relieve me.

Three days later, an email—
The baby opossum is doing okay.
Spinal injuries tend to take a long time to heal,
and we are hopeful and happy with his progress.

Some would say you are just a dumb animal,
not worth saving—but broken things can be redeemed,
and beauty is a hiss at dusk
in the middle of the road.

Convergence

On the banks of the Ardoch Burn,
in the shadow of Doune,
a thick-pelted otter lollops
up and over lichen-coated igneous
left dry in the cleugh.

I marvel at its slinky deftness,
its effortless, oily movement among the stones,
its back flexing to match the riffles,
lippering astride its hop-dive-curl-stretch—
lovely syncopation in walnut brown.
Then, finally, in mid hop-curl,
it is gone.

My father has made it halfway down
the slope that leads to the water's edge.
From there, I take his hand
and help brace his body,
so fragile now I barely feel
its weight against my arm.

Together, we reach level ground and pause.
We talk about the grey heron
we see wading in the river,
silent and precise in its quest for perch.
I tell him of the otter,
long and sleek and blink-swift.

My father says little—
a manifestation of his condition,
his neurologist tells me.
But I suspect he is thinking
about the otter with envy
as I offer my arm for ascension.

Magpies and Mortsafes

As I approach Flodden Wall, an archway of granite and moss,
a pair of magpies,
feathered deep purple-black with streaks of white,
call to one another in strident staccatos,
warning me not to get too close—
yet I can walk no other way but through.

Here, just beyond Greyfriars Kirk, in a clearing
ringed with granite headstones and mortsafes of rust-streaked iron,
under a name I cannot discern, I mark an inscription in French—
Dans la lumière il y a de l'espoir, and I find
I can think of no one but you.

Built centuries ago to protect the city from invasion,
the wall still stands as so many lie
within vaults and under plots of earth
that form a grid of countless intersections.

Standing among these monuments to loss,
I am Lear transfixed—
and the tablets mark not so much an end to me now
but a grasping upward, a reaching back into the world
toward someone loved and left behind.

I hear the magpies calling to one another again
from within an ancient beech tree, whose branches twist
in spirals upon spirals and out and out,
like my arms reaching for you, cleaving something to themselves,
wanting to hold it out into the air and allow it to breathe again.

Every name, inscribed on every stone, is yours.
Below the kirkyard, the roots of every tree conspire with the dead,
forsaking the ground, to write your name on everything,
everything.

On Thursday, you told me you wear only black.
Today, in this place of decaying stone and markers of the past,
I see only layers of the brightest auburn,
luminous against so many dark veils.
Today, surrounded by a thousand names that kaleidoscope into one,
I see only light.

Notes

The epigraph for *Dark Things Still* comes from Mary Oliver's "The Uses of Sorrow" included in her collection *Thirst* published by Beacon Press in 2007.

First Kiss: The quotation "the most passionate since the invention of the kiss" is a line from Rob Reiner's 1987 film *The Princess Bride.*

No Place for Freya: The epigraph comes from an online article published in August 2022 by Eurogroup for Animals.

Waiting in Winter: The epigraph for this poem comes from Mary Oliver's "Where Does the Temple Begin, Where Does It End?" included in her collection *Why I Wake Early* published by Beacon Press in 2005.

About the Author

Philip Andrew Lisi is a writer, teacher, and sometime actor. He holds degrees in English from Davidson College and North Carolina State University and recently completed an MFA program in creative writing at Arcadia University. A Best of the Net and Pushcart Prize nominee and Rash Award in Poetry finalist, he lives in Lancaster, Pennsylvania, with his family and their cantankerous Wichien Maat cat, Hazel. His work has appeared in a variety of literary journals and magazines, including *Broad River Review, Kelp Journal, Sky Island Journal, Third Wednesday Magazine,* and *Wild Roof Journal. Dark Things Still* is his first full-length poetry collection.

www.ingramcontent.com/pod-product-compliance
Lightning Source LLC
LaVergne TN
LVHW090535110826
845146LV00003B/1111
* 9 7 9 8 9 0 1 4 6 8 0 1 2 *